THERE'S A WITCH IN THE WORD MACHINE

for
all the witches

THERE'S A WITCH
IN THE WORD MACHINE

Jenni Fagan

First published in Great Britain in 2018 by
Polygon, an imprint of Birlinn Limited

Birlinn Limited
West Newington House
10 Newington Road
Edinburgh
EH9 1QS

www.polygonbooks.co.uk

ISBN 978 1 84697 463 2
eBook ISBN 978 1 78885 104 6

British Library Cataloguing-in-Publication Data
A catalogue record for this book is available
from the British Library.

Typeset in Verdigris mvb by Polygon, Edinburgh
Printed and bound by TJ International Ltd, Padstow

CONTENTS

There's a Witch in the Word Machine

There's a witch in the word machine
spell-casting:

dots, particles, atoms
elemental, bodiless,

a typing shell!

The nothing sky has no good intentions.
Go beyond it.

Timber wolves bay in testimony
as fingertips trail light:

argot, idiom, double-grave, slash-through

words have no pure notions . . .
they are flesh

strong and ventricle –
poison tipped arrows,

gouge them out

with a sharpened athame.
This is no thaumaturgy

(she can't leave the word machine)
astral lovers (as they are)

cannot be parted by logic or reason,

she brings no betrayal,
only incantations, divination,

sex magic
and a desire to crash the programme,

rewrite it as it should have
been.

Spell for Hope and Renewal

Take rain cold and sharp, the bite of wind,
two good claw marks, the estranged

ways of sunlight, bring common warmth,
and an idea of harmony, acceptance

of discord out there in all the great
beyonds and even, in the valleys.

Natural Born Itinerant

1.   Do not travel without poetry and by that I mean
         pen and soul.
2.   Know the road runs even when you are not allowed
         (that month / day / second / year) to devour
         its pictures from trains, and planes, scooters
         and rollerblades, skateboards and bicycles,
         or on foot, or even whilst dancing.
3.   Always find the place in each city with views – know
         the escape routes at all times.
4.   Have a child who is keen on becoming a nomad
         (just in case).
5.   Make home a place you can't remember.
6.   In between each heartbeat – try to find the promise
         of a familiar door.

Spell for One Who Dreams They are in a Vast Red Room

It was all red in there: walls, ceiling, door.
I was looking for a pot of beige
but I didn't have one, it was not legal to me and I'm always law
    abiding.
The room was red – not the poppy of your lips,
nor the cherry as you knot it,
with a pink, wet, tongue.
We're not talking claret or carmine or cardinal,
it didn't seem to be of the greatest importance,
it was plain and simple
(aside from the cornice and the ceiling rose)
– it was no damask,
it didn't taste vermillion,
it didn't slide down my thighs
bloody and against me.
It was no sanguine dream,
forget anodyne,
this was red, red, red!
Unchangeable red.
That room was waiting for me –
it was mine alone.

Backing Dancers of White Rabbits in Suits

Reality is a many-lensed construct,
don't blame it on white rabbits. There's a barn
by a river
by a valley
by a mountain
by a motorway
by a deep sky
by eternity
and it says scream if you want to go faster roll up, roll up!

You're in a wicker casket
while a heart shaped fire burns
and we will never lay spell
upon each other
but I miss the light
of the moon
on a stone floor,
two cats,
a lamp that looks
better squint,
nearby the structures protest too loud – whilst all the realities
ignore them.

Sunday Afternoon

I

Red leaves were
falling, the month you

left, time and mortality
duelled unseen,

while spirits visit
most on Hallows' eve,

they don't let me be
in any season.

My eyes that
day were sadder

than they've ever
been, there's no

way to get this
feeling out of me.

II

I won't say it is ok,
whisky can't cure it,

and I don't care
if time wants to heal

it, I don't want
another's touch.

I can barely speak,
silence is pouring

out of me – red
leaves were falling

the month you left
and each night

I lay awake
in the dark

in my bed.

III
There's tears
at time passing,

there is loss
and regret –

the reddest of
leaves

were falling,
the month

that you left.

Spell for the Futility of Longing

He won't come (often).
I've had seven

months of walking
on the string of a violin.

My feet are bloody
and my patience

long gone,
I must now step

into the chateau
of realism.

He won't come –
at any time, I'll know,

but when he does
he wants *l'amour*

my tongue, my mouth
open below him,

his desire is so much
he loses the power

to stand for a while
after and looks

at me with blue eyes
orange rimmed

and potentially
sociopathic

(at least a touch)
all looped

out on the precipice
of space and reason

but with love,
he touches.

I used to want him
(often) I lie

to myself
now that I don't,

a good witch
always banishes

the baneful,
for it sickens

body and soul.

Spell for Waking in the Museum of the Lost Generation

Dream of disappearing,
of leaving your lover,

telephoning him
from the far highlands,

the bells of Notre Dame
are taciturn

this morning
and your desire

for the passion of subversion
is strong

(always)
and you imagine

tongues
and cocks,

skin and salt,
sweat and perfume,

the old wood creaks
behind you,

in Shakespeare & Co.,
the dead poets

are glad you're in residence –
each morning,

you sing them songs.

Spell for Loneliness in Paris

Don't go looking for Rimbaud,
he would not entertain you.

The streets here will remind you only
of beauty and love, of first sights,

a man inspecting a tree,
his Panama hat

and his scar will be of some
comfort – but he can hear

your poet's clarity
your heart clangs

like the church bells
it chimes

and chimes
and chimes.

In the cafe, all alone
by Rue Saint-Sulpice

if that can be the name,
Parisian girls

take the swing of thin hips
as a given from Venus,

and we gather in the streets
to watch them –

we are all a part of a spectacle, which turns with its dark night
and in the morning

you are still sitting – a man sweeping the street
looks like your lover,

in another time – so long ago.

Spell Written in a Square

This
world
is
enough
to make your heart
hurt
all
the time.

An Old Fashioned Courtship

Your fingers under the snap of elastic
and over-washed lace,
you are beauty and grace –
our bodies are battlegrounds,
we advance and retreat.
You lay me down upon the tombstones
to see if my heart still beats –
we do it like witches
we do it like freaks,
we do it like we're gonna die in the morning,
like you've just served time, ten or twenty years –
you always did undo me at the seams,
this is love – sings the choir,
it's fucking lust – intones the priest,
you tip him the hat and get down on your knees –
they have countless ways to kill people like you and me –
it's preordained
we are unsavable as saints,
while your unrepentance is admirable it has to be said –
some questions – can only be answered in bed,
the lines around your eyes, you're brittle, and strange
never alarmed me –
your perversions and weirdness always kind of charmed me:
a degenerate sweetheart,
some kind of visionary
we get fucked up, fuck up and repeat –
they say there has to be agony
if there is ever to be ecstasy
fuck that shit,
I don't need absolution
just that you hold this heart – so carefully . . .
after all this time,
baby – it's you, fuck me.

I Fall in Love All Day

Next to Café de la Mairie
a man is searching,
searching, endlessly, the street
for something he has lost (it is his youth)
from now until the end of existence
it shall not
be found, nevertheless
he takes a seat
just in front of me, jiggles his knees,
taps on the table,
looks this way and that,
then this way again – so difficult it is
to sit – when time
has you trapped.

Spell for One Who Feels as if They Will at Any Second Take Flight

Barefoot, your least is to make time possible,
it is much – your heart.

Sand drifts, billows out to sea,

arms – cradle you
somewhere in memory,

rosebud knots
form at each shoulder

ache, to form wings
each and every night

grey, black and white feathers

flutter until sunrise
pink as a bitten lip

comes again to tempt
Earth's angels into flight.

My House is Not My House

My house is not my house since my lover
came around, kitchen walls that
stood impassive are now splayed
with the imprint of our fingertips.

Those stairs didn't hold the memory
of knuckles, I was never on my knees
by the pantry and that door – is not
just a space I walk through anymore.

My bed is the place where your arms
held me – safe as I've ever been,
we'd switch – fingers around throats,
pinned down wanton and delirious.

My house is not my house since my lover
came around. My bath holds the sound
of his voice, my floor is a place where I
cried surrounded by glow in the dark

balloons and was picked up and taken
upstairs and tucked in. I began to listen
always for your tread, in the end it was
just a thud of keys on the mat as you left.

Want

I have a terrible
craving

for him today.
Why are cravings always terrible?

They stamp on flower beds,
and hurt my mind.

I can't take them, nor
the news today,

for once,
don't let me near it,

I can still feel him
on the surface of my skin:

fingers
in my hair

his mouth,
turning my face around

to better
see him.

I have a terrible craving
for touch,

and it won't be sated
by cinnamon

or curses uttered by saints,
or backwards walking

nor biting my own knuckle hard
nor the softness of my bed.

This is a prison
I did not make,

and for all I know
his cravings for me

are already gone
and what I want

is a ghost,
a time where

in my bed we were happy
in the day hours,

strange to each other
yet so familiar.

Gertrude and Alice

Hold hands,
tell me a woman like me
(it is me)
with silver marks on my belly,
thighs that could crack
a man's neck in two
(should they need)
a stomach that carries the softness
of bearing a child
and a love of conversation, drink,
food, who sometimes deals with
stress by freebasing toast
and who has been asked by a make-up artist
when I am expecting
(but I am not)
and who's constantly
made to feel like any imperfect body
is the manifestation
of a personality defect
and I question ideas of perfection
so coveted as they were
by the Aryan race
and I question the culture of judgement
I do in fact judge it
and at some point every decent
human being has to say,
patriarchy is not welcome in my salon
(nor is its insistence on weakness)
I'm unwilling to play nice
to not intimidate

to act sorry
when I am not
to compensate –
to try and not scare the penis-bearers
when it is so easily done!

Gertrude
takes me back to sit among the art,
I'm her favourite
piece, even although I rarely smile.

I

Tasted you
in the must of books

that belonged
to a man

named George,
to Anais,

to Henry,
that were thumbed

by all who
sought them

I tasted you
in those books

I must in fact
taste you,

followed
by banana

with coriander,
not as satisfactory

in any way as your touch,
it was an odd

kind of mourning.

Spell for a Woman in Waiting

So he wants you
to be his woman in waiting

assigned you a role
that makes his reins

feel all leather,
ready to ricochet

his carriage
on a winter's morning,

the horse's nostrils
flare before humans

can hear the whip,
he wants you

to know what your role
is in comparison

to his, you can wait
for responses

of all and any kind,
he has exes to inform

(perhaps) or (not)
but possibly,

and that will take
many seasons

and if you say
this is not for you

that you live
in a permanent

state of conflict
and guesswork

(but it produces
no pretty blankets)

and this position
on his list

is not one you want
to pick

(the last of things he
must attend to)

(the top of his
addictions)

when you say
this is doing nothing

for your self esteem
that his lies are

stains he calls truths
because he will

never (say or not say)
what this is

or will be, or when he'll
arrive or who will ever know

(it will be nobody)
and when he shifts

uncertainty by the ounce
expects you to wait in for it

and when you
appear (finally) to be edging

down from the chariot
before the potential

of speed
and death,

he says –
don't rule this out,

I adore you,
my carriage has an open door,

for a woman-in-waiting,
but she will always

have to be
that way for me,

if she thinks freedom
is just another word

or that she has nothing
left to lose . . .

well – I cannot be
your woman

in waiting,
in secret,

in limbo,
in uncertainty,

my needs inferior to your
wants? I tried it until I began

to find my self respect
in the OBITUARY

section of the newspaper
every fucking morning!

I went back and took
out a full page ad,

poet with a broken heart
says take your shit back!

Do You Remember?

Do you remember the birds when we were children?
Do you remember skies
so bleached without colour
the only answer could be a nameless dread,
whale bones
on a stony beach,
do you remember kites,
and splinters,
the way you got that wound on your finger
only to keep pressing down
lest it forget to ache?

The Bones of the Witch's Tree

I don't know how not to want you,
your arms, your tongue,

old, gnarled, jaded,
I crave your touch, your soul

your love – I don't know how
to stop – wanting – you.

Or is it just that I want
love . . .

the bones of the witch's tree
are so bald and smooth,

the buds of spring
might as well not come –

I don't know how to
not want you

it is something I don't know
so for now I have to go.

I'll be back on a chopper,
I'll be peddling prophecy,

I'll be pure and ancient,
I'll be yours in sleep,

I'll let my heart know I listened,
did not ignore what it had to say,

the question is yours (not mine)
as to why it had to be this way.

Ode to Unconditional Love

If all I do is love you
if all I do is that,
if all I do is love you
if all I do is that .

If all I do is hold you
if all I do is that,
if all I do is love you
if all I do is that.

If I get just one love right
if there is only
yours to not get wrong,
when I am far

above you,
when my voice
has long since gone.
All I will do

even then is love you,
in this life just as true
in the next
I'd come back to this world

a billion times
over,
if that's all it took
to see you again.

Gringo's Whiskers

He burns them on a candle
lies on his back
an' snores.
Later he'll wake
kiss me with his nose,
he'll watch tennis
I'll make us chicken for tea
an' tell him again
he is the best
of all the Gringos
an' how grateful I am he never left
not when the moon
hammered on the window
for bone
or when the roof
double dared me
and the cartoon
became Monday
not when ghosts
came to stay
an' refused the living
at the door
not when sea
threw me to sky
or when the fridge
only held a microphone
not when I got back
from New York
and set the sky alight
held a three year chat with death

slept only
with spirits
an' sold rings of tin
for gold.

Hackney

He thinks about what shape thoughts are –
says that I am the colour blue
black-blue
he says I am the colour of lightening,
he says thoughts are the shape of fractals,
and when he turns away
as if I were
just a commodity,
trees stand tall in the parks of Rio,
and dogs in Hackney
still get walked.

Spell for Someone Eternally Restless

Firstly – don't count all the ways
in which you cannot settle,

perhaps in your skin,
in square rooms (certainly),

on the train
and before dawn,

in the middle of the night waking,
at the school pick-up,

in doctors' surgeries,
on train seats that face others,

on stage and in secret,
just think instead of how sneaker

laces tie so satisfyingly.

Living with Dharma

She thinks of the preposterousness of the body
with its lines and triangles
its hair
its design flaws,
its endless disappointments.

Tales of the Old Country

There never was a point where God
did not covet mortal women
with their nipples and filthy jokes,

the way they cut their men down
in the forests while singing to each other,
and how they laid them out like worry dolls

on the other side of the mountain.
They bitched to each other while they worked –
carried their holy, holy (some kind of a vase),

they didn't water anything
that would not grow,
they laced God's beard with acorns.

Their only unicorn slept easy in the clearing,
for there were no men to steal his ivory horn
to cut him wide open with a gut knife

and climb inside his warm body
and wear him like they tried
to do with most things – like they often did.

When the children came, born of acorns,
they were brown and sharp as the scythes
that cut down the first autumn's hay.

The women stacked those bales and lay
upon them under stars smoking and passing
biscuits they made (only ever in the shape

of moons). Quiet as ants they spoke
to each other, telling stories
of the old country – where men still live.

Spell for When You Cannot Breathe in Paris for a Day

The spell for this is hidden
in a vault,
by the eighteenth ventricle,
and without it there will be no option
but to be a woman who
looks to anyone else
to be Joan of Arc,
who does not appear to be a goldfish out of water
(one hopes)
but who is indeed this.
Think of Madonna
when she had a perm,
oxygen . . . ach, it comes and goes,
don't stop travelling
for this simple lack
of breathing.

Swan

Your fist
wears the whole of my body

and the tube is on the way and people are sitting on it –
your other knuckles

bandaged by my hair,
neck pulled all the way back –

do you remember swan?
do you remember how I loved you?

do you remember this?

Bangour Village Hospital

I was born here,
then a little while later I died.

Being born was something to do,
dying was something to do,

it was important –
to have something to do here.

After all these years.
After, all the lives I've lived!

Now I want to come back –
but they won't let me in.

We were refugees from reality.
Life escapees.

We knew what the worst thing was
so deeply in our bones

there could never
be any unknowing it.

They put a church in here.
There was a bell.

It tolled.
There was a holy man.

There was a shop.

There were green things in the outside world
and going there was helpful

but not beyond the end of the road.
Beyond the end of the road

there was judgment
and fear and anger.

People came from there,
wearing neat uniforms.

Everybody knew it.

Some of them had a kind hand.
Three did actually.

three had a kind hand but they also had an unkind hand –
those two hands often fought with each other – inside my body.

We had to be patient.
This was not a kind of dying.

Dying held no kindness
and we were labelled for patience.

They electrocuted
synaptic transmissions until we were all

forget-me-nots!
This was no metaphorical Sheol.

The church bell tolled
so the devil would know we were onto him

but he was so far down,
all the way down in my stomach like an apple pip

and I was born with that seed
my veins like branches –

like that it began to grow.

In 1906, it was 1906, in 1906
post came to the Edinburgh District Asylum.

There were people here for years before
but nobody says it.

Two years before that the builders had left
clean worktops and sink taps

that could be turned
and water would come out

and it was hot or it was cold
but never both, the first one turned

those taps so the rest of us could too.
They were the first ones.

They had no files.
Two years without an address,

it's not a place before a name
only a collection of walls

and scents, mostly Formica.
All of us were nameless.

Sometimes we shared a name
passed it around the wards at night

on a slip of sweetie wrapper,
Pressed it into each other's hands

when the nurses weren't looking.
We swallowed that name

with our tablets, each would fall
through emptiness

and land with an echo
at the bottom

of Bangour Village Hospital's well.
Things swam down there.

Things so terrible
I have never been able to shine

a torch, but the others did
which is why they didn't make it.

I was always being born
and dying

and being born again.
I decided to stop being born.

I decided to wear ugliness like fine silk pyjamas.

I'd just be in this skin
even if I never wanted it in the first place.

Who could be so ungrateful?
Uncertain bones still walk – some.

So it was we were given wreaths
to wear in our hair,

made of hope and true heart
but often laced with spiritual squalor

we decorated them with daisies
and we never fed the botanist who muttered

only about weeds. In 1918,
they brought in normal people to a new general hospital on our
    grounds.

We knew they were normal
because they told us so. They told each other too.

They had meetings in case
anyone was uncertain.

Just to be sure who was what,
it's good to be sure about these things.

We were us and they were them.
We were the others but they were unlovable to us!

They modelled Bangour on Altscherbitz.
Do you know it?

We were an asylum of village psychiatric.
Not village people.

One doctor played a harp
and sang about the preservation society.

There was a holy, holy workshop, a holy recreation hall,
it smelled like school-murk, dink-dank.

Each village held thirty.
There were chickens.

They called that patch a farm.
It did grow onions and also potatoes.

All faiths were welcome in the church but some
were more welcome than others.

We had incinerators.
We had a railway connection.

We had a library.
The railways left this place, it was cyclical as rebirth and decay.

They let us in here between the wars.
Then after 1945 we took it back for a good, long time.

We were crazy in a village in the eighties.
Your fashion was awful.

Our architect was Hippolyte Blanc.

He put an Edwardian Baroque hall at the centre of thirteen,
(it couldn'tbe twelve seeing as we were not a whole set of seasons)

and the church was Romanesque, the latter belonging to
H.O. Tarbolton. Nobody called him H.O. in public.

Our railway did not take us to the world beyond the tracks.

It was authorised by the Edinburgh and District Lunacy Board
to run one way only.

It brought coal and tablets: mountains of tablets
as big as the mountains of coal

and neat plastic fetishised needles
and fresh electric probes

and one day riding high on that train an electric machine to
shock us all. But machines in themselves

are not shocking.
It's the kind of people

who design them –
say one little boy pulls on a cat's tail,

drags it into the bus
tells his audience

see what will happen when I cut out its brain
with a scalpel?

They shut the railway soon after.
Even things coming in one way was a direction too many.

Static were the trees.
Static were the stones.

The house of God Stands Open to Thee Forever –
until it does not of course.

Some people were happy here
with trees of evil in their Gutula.

It was a place to come.
You can see that, can't you?

When rooms were unsafe
and street corners worse

there was always here to come and stand and know the trees and
    the dark
and the wards and the meds and the fear and the strange and the
    faces
old and new.

Now where is there?

One day they moved a wooden
building lest we think it were a fixed thing.

Now out there in the community it is all waiting lists.
Often not even places of bricks to go to.

Nothing.
Just a street corner.

Where is there now?

566 of ours had unmarked graves
right on this site.

Not on the cricket ground.
You can walk there but don't think we can't see you.

Lights out is coming again, in the end.
We all knew it would.

Lights out. Lights out.
Can you hear the bell?

Our dreams had dates with nightmares.
They took over the grounds until dawn.

We were not the war veterans who spent time here
broken but so brave

we were something to fear
or hide

or deny
we were always low on tobacco and Largactil.

We know soldiers roamed
those grounds at night

and all that was left of them
were hankies.

There were good nurses
and there were bad nurses,

so says every family.

Some went.
They all went.

But, many came back again and again.
We never left Ward 9 unmanned –

some feedback
you see

is best delivered from the grave.

You can't medicate a spirit.
You can't pinch it,

or electrocute it,
or drop water on its brain.

Most especially you can't help it.
We were so beyond all that.

We bided our time.
Those who died moved into Ward 9 so they would never leave us.

All the nurses were too scared to go in the patients' lift.

We still had hearts
and they were beating

but when all that stopped
we'd join Ward 9.

It was somewhere to go.
Having somewhere to go was important.

The voices nurses heard were not ours
and they knew it

and we all knew collectively that one day only birds would live here.
In these empty wards.

Each bird chirping.
Nesting.

Little bird-babies with gilded golden cages
around their black hearts.

They give us no silence.

Spell for a Stomach that Cannot Keep Food

The pain of gnarl
and bone of discontent

the twig of disease
the opposite

of peace,
the oscillation of atoms

the beam
from dark matter

the cloves hoofed
and heavy

the wait
and dislocation,

the wary,
suspicion

of others intent –
all this can be soothed

with love,
flying dreams

slippery elm
and much less gin.

She is Not the Cat's Mother

She is half Sicilian
her face
in the morning
dim
is golden
her body above me
is all things
beautiful
and free
and when she talks
all I think of is her tongue
her lips
how her kiss feels to me
she drove her car
into a dairy truck,
picked me up
brittle with wrecked hands
I love,
to touch
to run my breath across her skin
for twenty years I thought of her,
as she did me,
(we never even said)
and now I imagine sitting with her on a plane,
sleeping with her under a glass domed bed
aurora and milky way
for covers,
fire
and chat,
touch and taste

cigarette and coffee,
I'd have done anything at all to make her smile
when she felt so bad
but still looked at me that way.

Spell for God

This is how we do, we do –
in the middle of the night,
God and I
play chess
(long past last orders)
just him and me sitting at the bar
all the angels cry,
when we meet like this
I don't tell him how much I want to go back
to the kingdom of light
instead I beat him at chess,
send a thousand arrows
wrapped in want
(a good shot)
(I shoot well for a girl)
he wears them like a fucking
porcupine.

Spell for Bellevue Street

I'm waiting for you.
You know where.

You know when.
The window in the bathroom

has flowers on the glass
I hate, it's been this way

since 1930, the sun shines
through them, or the grey

I'm waiting for you,
my heart beats too fast

you open the door
and neither of us needs to

speak, our imprint
began on Bellevue Street.

You Know

I want to cry with you.

I never want to hurt you,
I always want you to be okay.
I'm willing to walk away,

if that's what it takes.

Spell for Someone Who Had Not Dreamt of a Unicorn Lately

Pick up a clay teapot
unpainted

do green strokes
the sea refuses

to know you,
how it swells

how it calls,
you are all anxiety

and glass bones
as you paint onto clay

unicorn tears
later you'll amuse yourself

by pouring them as tea,
whilst in another country

your lover once again
ignores you.

It's the Silence That Gets to You

Where before there were fingers and thumbs
that line
when he smiled
at the left of his mouth
where there were texts coming in,
knocks on the door,
bicycle on the path,
footsteps on the stair
your voice low in the dark,
eyes in the light,
creaks on the bed,
guttural
shudders
the murmur
the arms around you,
how peaceful it felt
how much like home,
the promises,
the secrets –
now
there is only silence.

Spell for Something to Covet

I
A gothic church.

II
A gothic island.

III
A vintage hearse
        and
    fields of poppies.

O.C.D.

The brain fucks itself
in circles.

In circles.
In circles.

The brain fucks itself in circles.
In fucking circles.

It's fucking sick.

It fucks itself in circles
designed

solely to kill,
it fucks you in circles

until you are truly ill.

It's invisible
to others, the relentless

bully of O.C.D. – it circles
you in circles

especially when you've
learnt to live

with it, live
with it, live with

it, even when you've
learnt to circle

it, it is still a fucking circle
and all it wants to do

is kill
your soul in circles, in circles

in circles, it fucks
you in circles

it always will.

Spell for Someone with a Feather Tattoo and Illicit Thoughts

First – you need a lover
light of touch

yet aggressive
in delivery

when required –
you need the tilt

from heart to hip
you need one

(at least)
who will not let it go.

Spell for Earthbound Angels

So far from light
you crave

dear one, how much you crave,
taste, touch

and the world of men went to war
against you,

and here you are
unarmoured

and being asked to love
to share your lust

the want you have to soar
is never far

you had to come to live on this earth
so far from home,

when he takes you in his arms
how susceptible

are you
(who came only from a place of love, of pleasure)

– you arrived here
full of want

for the intensity
of lust,

you are never allowed
to forget

the heart splitting,
soul yearning

for a place –
you cannot remember,

or forget.

St Bert

The desire to please a society
that needs its girls
coltish, but asks them to take part
in weakening contracts
to achieve the angularity of acceptance.

I wish to tell them
they are bound by no aesthetic,
though the dizzying
promise of adoration
is a master all of its own.

Worship comes for every shape
do what suits you
but get strong!

It's all good, the seal, the colt
but when I think of beauty lately
I think of this woman with dark eyebrows
and a nose hoop
unshaven and fat and stunning

in her way of inhabiting
her body,
luminous eyes,
cream-tea skin,
I think of her often – in particular her smile
and she makes me feel so fucking good.

I Want to Be the Kind of Woman

I want to be the kind of woman
made from the whispers of trees,

one who has been all the way down
buried underneath the leaves

I want to be the kind of woman
assassins refuse to take contracts for –

and angels go into therapy for
and long term felons always love her like

a daughter, or a light on the shore,
some sentences are served – unseen

I want to be the kind of woman who on her worst
days finds it in her to dance, who defies

the blackbird but later they trade smokes,
one who has slept in fire and swam in meteors

played dagger roulette with mermaids
and refused to spit on her slit wound

and who would not trade her pound of flesh
even when they took it and said they owned it

and said they'd bring unspeakable horrors,
most especially not even then.

I want to be the one who walks out the door
and when she feels her life is over

and there is no hope and she is ruined and broke
picks up nails and a hammer, shuts down the coffin,

traces the scars of her heart and carries
on regardless, through every kind of madness

so much – nobody could ever believe
who doesn't compromise on a soul mate

because loneliness is life
and she can smile perfectly well all on her own Sénor,

in the cold, hard, night –
I want to be the kind of woman

who stands tall, who overcomes
and even if no one else does,

knows how she is extraordinary –
I want to be that kind of woman,

I want that woman to be me.

On Loving Men with Beards

I loved the first man
a man
who was crusty
and chemically unavailable
and he blinded
me with the depth of the hit,
infatuation
to this day
can floor me
for a day or two at best,
what a load of shit,
it can curve ball any one of us
at any given time
and there's no deadline on it,
months, years, moments when your heart
knows it is just
a beat (or street) away
from the most amazing
sex (never mind the love)
when you get that yearn to touch
another
whose
radar is sending out signals
like a lighthouse
far down the shore
on the stormiest
night
and you're not even sure
if you're making
that light appear from sheer
desire
to be touched

to have and to hold
to fuck
and be fucked
and somewhere even further back
a place
where you wouldn't even leave a note
– to love
and be loved
and all the scholars
are sending you messages
saying, *focus*
your shit, Fagan!
but when you want – you want,
when that want creeps
in under the door
because it just happened to see the light
as you read
past the witching hour,
while you refuse
to allow
the idea
of going to those depths with someone,
to letting them in,
to be the one who knows you
and when
all reason tells you
to forget it
– so of course it's all you think of
that touch,
from your lovers hand
a need to feel loved, and in return to love
to hold and be held
to fuck and be fucked
and your heart is so raw

from the loss
of losing those you adored
and you are trying
to let your soul split wide open
with that pain
and grief
rather than close it down
and this sheer ill-making agony is
where you once again understand
why poets
and pen-pushers
and preachers
and ponies
and purists
and perverts
and the pretty
and the putrid
and the lovelorn
and the hopeless
have died for this –
and from this,
for want of it
from lack or too much,
from getting love
and finding
it has later
been taken back,
and over all the years
there have been
beards
and non-beards
and eyes
and arms
and love

and disdain
and loathing
and the ache
of knowing that all those versions
of love were only transient
and that stepping
out of bed
this
morning
at a time where I know all the ways
I can (and have) learnt to break
and repair
like my psyche
is a shitty television repair shop
and I am the mad scientist
who can fuse
the red wire with the blue
to bring forth
light
and sound
now – when I am at my most vulnerable
because I know what fragility
has to say about Sunday,
at this moment
I can't take it
so he sends a text
while I am stepping out of bed,
a thunderbolt
terror
because while there's been
convincing
dress rehearsals along the way,
and true
there has been love,

I'm not sure I can take this road again,
at a time when
I know myself so wholly
and have shut myself off so far,
for safety,
and to feel it this intensely makes me feel
like puking –
I still want you so much.

We Are Edinburgh

We beat
drums made of bone

we raise the dead,
they sit at our tables,

are still loved
in our beds,

they walk these cobbled streets
my friend,

we do (and do not) forget.

I Do Know This

I'd fuck you better
if I left you.

It's why I leave you at least once a week, or so.

It's not true,
we know it doesn't need any other edge,

I leave you because of your insistence that I do.
You'd say it was me.

You'd say it so.
There's a reason you need me to repeatedly come back

and then go.

The First Time

You were so
awkward
you were losing your cool,
sitting on my back,
changeable as the human tide,
I know what
happened that night,
you know,
we never were the same
again
you ran from my door within minutes
after, fled
whilst I sat down slightly amused,
and dazed,
and hurt,
and lonely,
to watch Maggie play secretary.

Addict

The body wants,
it wants and it wants and it wants and it wants
if you give it what it wants
it will never let you be.

Sentient Being

Dressed
tolerated
cleaned
sanitised
sex is in the cells,
deny it at your peril.

It Wasn't Nice the Way You Conducted the Orchestra

Who were you before you became a saint?

You insisted your every
action

was only
love and kindness,

what a load of fucking shite
your actions

served yourself,
they served your fucking life,

then you'd shout . . . how dare you ever say I
gave you anything

but love?
You – who speaks to me of delusion!

Whilst I, had to wrap up my darkness
in linen, in secret

lay it out on the grass
of a nearby park

it soaks up the moon's good rays,
and I wear it the next day

when you
have calmed down,

and begin to (not) hear me again.

It Doesn't Always End Well

When I was a girl
I would bathe in the river
when I didn't have somewhere to be
or when I couldn't live
in a place
or when I just had to go
and be where nobody knew where I was,
bare feet sliding over algae
on pebbles,
they were the knobbled bones of the river's trajectory
and I'd lay down to be cleansed by rapids –
wish for a gap between
my teeth –
wonder what people
who looked
like me
would look like
or what people related to me
would sound like
and if the next place would be for a month
or a year, or a week
a treachery – I could
never rest easy,
how I wish I could grow up to be
someone
who could tell that girl – it was all
going to turn out
all right,
but it doesn't always
end well
and I'm not there yet.

Responding to Life in a Secret Squirrel Universe

Living in a universe
add infinitum

without explanation . . .
is problematic

for humans,
all the tall tales

made up don't seem
to have helped

value must be placed
solely on existence

and goodness,
taking care first

of the planet,
and each other

as all we must
achieve.

Death in Sednaya

There are places where thinking can kill.

Where a boy's ears –
are more able than his eyes.

A trial can take a minute!
He has murdered no soldiers.

In the seconds
before execution,

his bare feet (once kissed by his mother)
scuff and his fingers grab

onto the shirt
of the man in front (like he did as a toddler to his brother)

as he walks the train,
he thinks of his mother's smile.

While tyrants practise murder
in golden beds

in silence,
he mops up the red.

Fear descends all depths!

This is the true shame of humanity.
As he walks that train he remembers

how his cousin felt in his arms
starved as he was to death

a bird in flight, how he envied
that release from hunger and thirst, but more so

from thoughts and memories,
unbearable, his executioner will leave this place tonight

he prays for his soul, as he lowers his head.

Holding Yourself with Dignity

I was on the 176,
going back home to Peckham,

and there was a sign
spray-painted thirty feet tall,

I MISS YOU

I remember it
from all those years ago

and I want to go out tonight –
with red spray paint,

do the entire road
outside your tenement

set something on fire,
go for a joyride,

but instead I say nothing . . . to you
try to make great art,

I love my child,
listen to music loud

steel my spine like a poker
player in Cape Town,

gambling's all I've got left
and whether I cry . . .

or not each morning (I do)
I'll never beg –

not for love,
or golden pears

nor will I sharpen toxic arrows,
I'm a woman

with a wolf on her arm,
and I hold myself well.

Spell for Angels in Paris

Ring the bells (when you wake)

in glory,
in delirium,

ring, ring, ring
the bells!

I'm sleeping in a bookshop
waking across from Notre-Dame,

the dead and undead
writers are muttering,

the bells, the bells!
I'm barefoot

into the shower
out there it's all peals and intent and traffic

the lovers and lovelorn
must wake!

Coffee – comb tangled in hair,
hammers strike brass,

even heaven
splits her atoms,

I'm hungover
and happy

as the angels of Paris
send a cease and desist

to dreamers,
to dreaming – they must all hear this,

it is time to rise
we heart beaters . . .

it has been decreed – stamped,
issued by angels

in Paris.

ACKNOWLEDGEMENTS

I'd like to thank the people that allow me time to chat and be, seeing the world as a poet is not easy even if you play the smallest violin on Earth.

Shakespeare & Co. in Paris, who had me stay in their extraordinary bookshop. I found a spiritual home – the museum of the lost generation, a residency that inspired me whilst writing these spell poems and thinking of all the great writers who spent time in the shop or near there: Anais Nin, Henry Miller, Gertrude Stein and Rimbaud, this collection owes a debt to that time and space. Thank you Sylvia Whitman, thank you Adam Biles.

There are those who I don't impose my poetry on but rather my skiff-schizzle, skullduggery, my broken heart and conflict, who are patient and listen: Mrs Kane, Jane, Ewan Morrison, Irvine, Dorothy Allison, Kate McQuaid, Kevin Williamson, Bonnie-Jo Campbell, Kayus, Tom Leonard, Tracy Bohan, Alan Bett, Rowan, Lynsey May, Nate Krenkel, Jane, Jim Loach, Mr Conn, Mr Ray's Wig World, Rob, Ryan, Ever Dundas and more. Some of you I rarely see, some I talk to all the time, some of you encourage me at just the right moment, it all helps to keep me going.

Edward Crossan at Polygon, who has developed a great eye for an edit, who is straightforward in his line notes and who I am glad to work with again on my poetry, also to all at Birlinn who have put out such a beautiful book, my thanks.

Tracy Bohan my agent, I still hope to impress you!

David Balfour, I miss you, Shirley Allison, I miss you, Gringo, Quita and the ancestors, my gratitude to you.

Boo, you are the one who I am utterly grateful for, I hope you always know how much I love you.

To the lovelorn and the loveless, to the loved and the insecure, to the bored and the crazy, to the desperate and terrified, to the hopeful, to the brave, to all of you – I hold out some poetry, may it wilt less than flowers.